My First Fast Car Book

Ticktock

Supercars

The McLaren F1 was the fastest car ever when it was first made in 1992. Even though McLaren stopped making them in 1998, it is still one of the fastest cars in the world today.

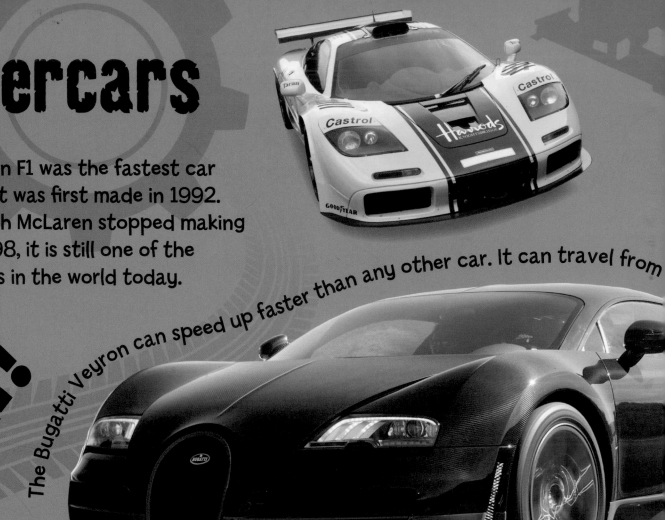

Brrm!

The Bugatti Veyron can speed up faster than any other car. It can travel from

From March 2007 to July 2010 the SSC Ultimate Aero was the fastest car in the world with a top speed of 257mph.

LaFerrari is Ferrari's first hybrid car. It was first made in 2013.

The super fast Koenigsegg Agera R has a hard roof that can be removed for open-top driving. It can reach 273mph.

Vroom!

0 to 60mph in just over 2 seconds.

In 2009 Porsche made the 9FF GT9-R. Only 20 were ever made and each one was made slightly different so that no two would be the same.

The Saleen S7 is a hand-built American supercar made from carbon fibre. Its engine is right behind the driver.

Ferrari LaFerrari

LaFerrari is Ferrari's most powerful road car, with a top speed of about 220mph. First made in 2013, it replaces Ferrari's previous supercar, the Enzo.

The body of LaFerrari is made from lightweight carbon fibre.

LaFerrari's huge engine is at the back of the car, over the rear wheels. As the car drives, air flows in through vents to keep the engine cool.

LaFerrari is Ferrari's first hybrid vehicle. This means it uses special batteries to power the car as well as a traditional gasoline engine.

LaFerrari costs nearly £1.1million and only 499 cars were built. These were all sold well before Ferrari even started making them!

Ferrari is a famous Italian car maker. They are often red because red is the racing colour of Italy.

Like all supercars, the front of LaFerrari is shaped so that air can easily flow over it, which makes the car go faster.

Bugatti Veyron

With a top speed of 253 mph, the Bugatti Veyron is one of the fastest road cars in the world.

To reach 253 mph the driver has to insert a special key, slowing the car to 220 mph.

The Bugatti Veyron has a spoiler that

brrm!

The inside of the Veyron is very comfortable, with thick leather covering the steering wheel and seats.

The engine of a Bugatti Veyron is more powerful than most Formula One cars.

Four new tyres costs around £23,500!

The Veyron Super Sport is Bugatti's record-breaking model, with a top speed of 267mph. It costs nearly £1.7million.

whoosh!

McLaren F1

McLaren first made the F1 in the 1990s. For seven years it was the fastest road car in the world, with a top speed of 241mph.

The driver sits in the middle of the car, like in a racing car.

The inside of the engine is covered in gold foil. This is to stop heat from the engine damaging other parts of the car.

The McLaren F1 has three seats – one in the front for the driver and two in the back for passengers.

McLaren are famous for making Formula One racing ars. Theu use some of

Like many super cars, the McLaren F1 has 'butterfly'
doors which open upwards and outwards.

On the Track

A car that has been altered to have a large, powerful engine and bright paint is typically known as a 'hot rod'.

A drag race sees two vehicles race side by side along a short, straight track. The winner is usually the car with the fastest acceleration.

The 24 Hours of Le Mans is a race in which three drivers take turns to race a car continuously for 24 hours, covering a total distance of over 3100 miles.

In October 1997, Thrust SSC broke the World Land Speed Record. It reached the amazing speed of 763 mph!

Formula One cars compete in a series of Grand Prix races, which are held all over the world.

More than 1500 NASCAR races are held at over 100 tracks across the United States and Canada each year.

NASCAR

Stock car racing is one of America's most popular motor sports. It is more commonly known as NASCAR.

NASCAR (The National Association for Stock Car Auto Racing) organises all the races and tests the cars to make sure they are as safe as possible.

The main car manufacturers that take part in NASCAR are Ford, Chevrolet and Toyota.

Daytona 500 is the most popular NASCAR race of the year. It is always the first race of the Sprint Cup Series season.

NASCAR cars are very different from road cars. Almost every part of a NASCAR is handmade.

The driver's last name is shown on the windshield and bright sponsorship logos cover the bodywork.

Formula One

Formula One, also known as F1, is the most popular type of motor racing in the world. Car makers spend millions to make their Formula One cars better than everyone else's.

Inside the driver's helmet are headphones so that he can talk to the rest of the team.

zoom!

The wheels are changed up to three times during a race.

In Formula One, pit stops are for fuel and for changing the wheels. This is done by a team of about 20 people.

For protection, the driver wears special fireproof clothes.

Formula One cars drive at very quick. They are able to go from 0 to 100mph in about 4 seconds.

Brrm!

The front wing is close to the ground, so that the air rushing over it pushes down and keeps the wheels on the track.

Classic Cars

The Mercedes Benz W125 was designed to race in the 1937 Grand Prix season. It was the fastest and most powerful Grand Prix car of its time, with a top speed of 193mph.

In 1965 the Mini won every racing competition it entered. It won a total of 17 rallies around the world including the famous Monte Carlo Rally.

Made in 1962, the AC Cobra was a British sports car with an American engine.

Brrm!

'Muscle cars' like this Ford Mustang were American, 2-door cars with very powerful engines.

Vrooom!

The Jaguar E-Type is one of the most famous cars in history. Over 70,000 E-Types were made and sold between 1961 and 1974.

In 2012, the Ferrari 250 GTO made in 1962 became the world's most expensive car. It sold for £23million!

Jaguar E-Type

The Jaguar E-Type is a British sports car which was very popular in the 1960s.

When it was first made, the Jaguar E-Type cost just £2097. They are worth a lot more today!

The E-Type's number plate was printed on a sticker because Jaguar thought it would spoil the look of the car.

Honk!

The long bonnet is one of its most famous features.

The Jaguar E-Type had a top speed of 149mph. There were no speed limits on the roads in the 1960s so the owners could drive as fast as they liked!

The large, heavy bonnet opened at the front of the car.

When they were first made, the E-Type had a button to start it, instead of a key.

Ford Mustang

The Ford Mustang, first made in 1964, is one of the most popular American cars ever.

The first Ford Mustang cars had four seats so that they would still appeal to young families.

The Ford Mustang was one of the first cars to come with many options. People could choose from different body styles, seats and paintwork.